Babies & Toddlers
FOR *MEN*

101 Tips

649.122081

Mark Woods

Babies & Toddlers for Men: 101 Tips

This first edition published in 2012 by White Ladder, an imprint of Crimson Publishing Ltd, Westminster House, Kew Road, Richmond, Surrey, TW9 2ND

Content in this book has been previously published in *Babies & Toddlers for Men* © Mark Woods, 2012

British Library Cataloguing in Publication Data

A catalogue record for this book is available from the British Library.

ISBN 978 1 90828 131 9

Typeset by IDSUK (DataConnection) Ltd

Printed and bound in the UK by TJ International Ltd, Padstow, Cornwall

To Sarah and the boys, 101 kisses.

Introduction

In a world where unloading the dishwasher has become a Herculean task requiring formidable levels of patience and fortitude, this little book represents the digestible face of fatherhood.

Taking the best bite-sized nuggets of information from the more meal-like *Babies & Toddlers for Men* this little book aims to bring you morsels of parenting wisdom harvested from a number of sources.

I'm not one of them though.

I don't claim to be an expert father and my wife certainly doesn't see me in that light either – what my children think only time will tell of course.

What I've done though is speak to scores of new dads and read everything there is to read about fatherhood – from surveys to manuals – to come up with a useful collection of tips which will help you not only enjoy your new role in life but also avoid a few of the pitfalls your predecessors have come across along the way.

Covering the first three years of your children's life the tips are in chronological order and touch on a vast array of the new issues you'll come across now that you are literally the daddy.

In hospital
and
0-3 months

1

Your family needs you

Be there as much as you can for the short but sometimes stressful stay in hospital.

Your partner will be grappling with a whole world of immediate challenges including establishing breastfeeding (much more on that to come); trying to figure out just when she is meant to rest; wondering what the hell to do with the alien-like umbilical cord stump; or, in many cases, just coming to terms with the reality of being a mother.

Night time can be especially tough and often even lonely for your partner after you've been turfed out on your ear at 10pm or so. It's a good idea to keep your mobile on overnight in case she needs to talk and arriving, cavalry-like, as soon as you're allowed back in the morning will go down well after a tough evening.

2

Exams already

The Apgar test, devised by the eponymous Dr Virginia Apgar, has been standard practice since the 1950s and the midwife will carry it out just by watching your baby's colour, breathing, behaviour, activity and posture, with each of the five factors then given a score between 0 and 2.

A perfect 10 out of 10 is obviously what every new parent wants to hear, but in reality an 8 or a 9 is still great news, a score between 5 and 7 means your baby is in fair condition but may require some help with breathing. Your midwife may vigorously rub your baby's skin or give him some oxygen if this is the case.

Newborns that score under 5 are considered to be in poor condition and are often placed on a special unit, which looks a bit like a doner kebab grill, where heat, light and oxygen is on tap to help warm them up and aid breathing. A paediatrician will also be called to help with initial treatment and decide on the best course of action.

3

Very special care

If your baby ends up in a special care ward, try your best not to fret too much.

These units are amazing places that will do everything in their considerable power to help your baby get healthy enough to leave hospital. Don't be afraid to ask questions and most importantly find out what all the beeps and machines are really early on so they don't intimidate you.

It will feel beyond awful leaving hospital without your precious bundle, but if your baby does happen to be poorly there is no safer place for them to be.

4

The aftermath

There's no nice way of saying this, but new mothers bleed a lot after they have given birth.

It's not the sort of thing that mums say to mums-to-be but it happens and you should be ready for it. This bleeding is called lochia and it's how the body gets rid of the lining of the womb after birth. The blood may come out in gushes and include clots, or flow more evenly like a heavy period, and more often than not it will change colour from the initial bright red and become lighter as the uterus heals and returns to its normal size.

Your partner may bleed for as little as two to three weeks or as long as six weeks.

5

This is your moment

Even though it is quite obvious that a Caesarean is major surgery in every sense of the word the after-effects and the pain it causes can still take a newly babied couple by surprise.

It can hurt to cough, to laugh, to shuffle around in bed, to do almost anything in fact. It's tough and it's down to you to help make it better by taking some of the strain of new motherhood on your broad shoulders, even if they are hunched through fatigue.

6

The baby blues

After such a crescendo of emotions and hormonal upheaval suffered by your partner, it's inevitable that there will be, for want of a better phrase, a comedown after the birth.

It's estimated that something like 80% of new mothers experience this crash back down to earth – sometimes called the baby blues – and it's thought to be linked to hormonal adjustments being made by the body, which take place two to four days after the baby is born.

7

Postnatal depression

One in four mums will suffer from postnatal depression (PND).

The existence of the baby blues muddies the waters slightly, but the medical advice is clear when it comes to distinguishing between the two. While the baby blues are short-lived and often disappear without treatment, the opposite is true of PND.

8

How did she do that?

Ben, father of two:

"Once your wife has a baby I don't think any rational man can look at the fairer sex again without thinking 'Hats off to you'.

"If men had children, Caesarean sections would have been invented before the wheel."

9

I know that face

In these early days after birth, your baby's specialist subject is ... the face.

In fact you'll catch your little one staring you down at any given opportunity and this intent study is their way of memorising your features so the people who are legally responsible can be indentified immediately should any litigation be required at a later date.

10

Nappily ever after

Your baby will be weeing up to 18 times a day and could be pooing anything up to seven times daily.

You will also become an expert on both colour and consistency of number twos.

In the early days, a newborn's poo tends to be thick and dark green in colour thanks to her proto-poop called meconium. As she starts to feed properly though you will often be confronted on opening the nappy by yellowish matter which has more than a passing resemblance to chicken korma.

11

Magic moments

There's something magical about the few days between when your first baby is born and when mother and child finally arrive home.

You feel elated and proud and special and why not? You are.

Milk it and enjoy every minute. If you have a second baby, it will still be an amazing moment but you'll have another youngster in need of some care and attention at home too, so make the most of these early amazing days, no matter how busy you are.

12

Never a dull moment

Like the earliest people on the planet, you now live in a world of firsts: the first bath, the first cry you can't calm, the first smile – they just keep on coming and each one represents a challenge or a moment of joy (often at one and the same time) that will grab your undivided attention like you would not believe.

What's key to remember is that everyone goes through the same steep, steep learning curve with their first baby – you are far from being alone.

13

Last orders

The Department of Health's recommendation for feeding infants is that exclusive breastfeeding for the first six months is the best approach. The department's own Infant Feeding Survey though painted a picture of a reality in sharp contrast with that ideal.

While 76% of mothers said that they wanted to breastfeed at the very start of their pregnancy, just one week in, the number exclusively doing so was down to 45%. By six weeks the figure had dropped to 21% and at the four-month mark just 7% of babies still had breastmilk as their sole sustenance.

By six months the figure was, in the words of the survey, negligible.

All of which tells us – breastfeeding can be very tough indeed.

14

Milk monitor

Should your partner try the breastfeeding route you can't guarantee a pain-free experience for her of course, but you can make a tangible day-to-day difference when she is attempting to make it work.

Is she comfortable? Does she have a drink and a snack to hand (breastfeeding seems to bring on an instantaneous killer thirst and major hunger pangs)? Has she got somewhere warm and quiet to focus on the task in hand?

They are small touches, but they can all help make it work.

15

Don't be shy

Despite both your best efforts things sometimes don't go well on the feeding front. But help is at hand.

Talking to community midwives, or ideally asking a breastfeeding specialist if there's one in the area to come round and help out is a good idea.

There's also the National Childbirth Trust breastfeeding helpline on 0300 330 0771 and the NHS national breastfeeding helpline on 0300 100 0212 – both of which can hook you up with a specialist breastfeeding counsellor quickly.

If you don't ask, you won't get and it can make all the difference.

16

The T word

Thriving is the name of the game for your little one in these first few weeks and months as they feed and grow, grow and feed.

If things aren't going as they should be there are some tell-tale signs to look out for.

If your baby is feeding at least six to eight times a day that's a very good sign as is the fact that the act of breastfeeding is painless for your partner – bleeding nipples aren't the way it's meant to be.

Wet nappies are another key indicator – once she's past five days old or so your baby should have at least six to eight wet nappies every 24 hours, and the wee itself should also be pale and relatively odourless.

Poo on the other hand should be a yellowy mustard colour if breastfeeding is the method of choice in your house, whereas bottle-fed poos are a paler yellow to tan colour.

Welcome to your new world.

17

Lotta bottle

If you've decided to go down the formula route, rather than being the social pariahs or, god forbid, failures you may consider yourselves, the figures show that you are in the majority.

So give yourselves a break and crack on.

18

The bap app

Colin, father of two:

"Breastfeeding was a nightmare to begin with. My wife suffered terrible cracked nipples, bleeding, infections, the lot. To her credit though she pushed through and ended up feeding for seven months.

I felt so helpless during the tough times – the hardest thing was not knowing how much milk baby was getting and how much was left in the boob . . . if only there was a gauge to let you know how much is left . . . maybe someone will design an app for that!"

19

Little and often

Newborn babies sleep a lot – up to 18 hours a day for the first few weeks and 15 hours a day by three months.

Sounds great, what's all the fuss about?

Thing is, despite the impressive overall amount of kip, for the first few months they rarely sleep for more than three or four hours at a time, day or night.

20

Grey, pink and blue matter

Boys' and girls' brains develop differently from the start in a very physical sense.

A boy's brain develops from the back – the doing part – towards the front – the thinking part, whereas a girl's brain develops in the opposite direction.

What that means is that boys develop their physical abilities before they start to think about them.

Sounds familiar.

Girls, however, develop more of their thinking and language skills first, which accounts for at least some of the reason why girls seem to race ahead when the time for school comes around.

21

So tired

Never ever turn down the opportunity of sleep.

Ever.

If you can convince yourself that each blink you do constitutes a nano-kip as well that's even better.

22

SIDs check list

Cot death, also known as SIDS – sudden infant death syndrome – mostly occurs in babies under six months. There is a widely accepted set of steps which can help keep your baby safe.

- Both of you cut out smoking in pregnancy and once the baby is born don't let anyone smoke in the same room as your baby.

- Place your baby on their back to sleep, not on the front or side.

- Do not let your baby get too hot, and keep your baby's head uncovered while they sleep.

- Place your baby with their feet to the foot of the cot, to prevent them wriggling down under the covers.

- Never sleep with your baby on a sofa or armchair.

23

Baby talk

In recent years the 'science' of actually being able to interpret what each type of baby cry means has moved on. The Dunstan Baby Language system for instance claims to have isolated each cry to a remarkable degree and lists the different sounds as:

Neh: I'm hungry

Owh: I'm sleepy

Heh: I'm experiencing discomfort

Eh: I have wind

Eairh: I have lower wind

Ey Wassup: I've been allowed to watch too much telly.

24

Keep calm and carry wet wipes

Always remember the three Ps – Preparation Prevents Pootastrophy.

A fully stocked changing table is a beautiful thing because once you open the Pandora's box of a full nappy, putting a lid back on it again while you try to find some baby wipes is not an easy thing to do.

Also when you do open things up, try to use the inside front part of the nappy itself to get the first wipe in. It will collect a very decent amount of poo from the soft little bottom of your cherub and leave you just the detritus to deal with.

The fear of your little one getting their hands in their own doings as you do the clean-up lives with all of us at every nappy change. You're not truly a dad until you have a face full of something nasty.

25

Just to see you smile

Your baby's first proper social smile can occur as early as four weeks after birth – and after the month or so you and your partner will likely have had, a little bit of a reward will be gratefully received.

As ever, the timings of this joyous happening can vary a lot so don't worry that you have spawned a mini-Morrissey if you don't get belly laughs when you're expecting them. If, though, you are lucky enough to see a smile even earlier than the four-week mark, don't let any sour-faced fool dismiss it as wind – smile right back and let the love in.

26

The travel cot conspiracy

Just to get this straight, every time is like the first time you put a travel cot up.

After an hour of push-me pull-you nonsense and with your baby's bedtime approaching at a frightening speed you gird your loins, pull up the middle and launch a surprise attack on the insurgent outer arms.

Still a floppy mess.

Reinforcements are needed – don't worry about who, anyone in the house will do – because the moment they approach, your travel cot enemy will sense that humiliation is almost complete and will become putty in their hands, gently complying to their every movement.

Swines.

27

The one without the boobs

If you feel your nose being put slightly out of joint by the closeness of the bond between mother and child, know this: your time will come.

In this initial spell it's easy to feel a bit of a spare part where the baby is concerned, but it's vital to remember that every cuddle you give and every gaze you hold is working to cement you as one of the two most important people in this little person's life.

Months 4-6

28

How nippers nap

As the little one grows she will gradually sleep more during the night and less in the day and at this stage, on average, she will be sleeping twice as long at night as in the day – or so the story goes.

Her daytime naps gradually coalesce to become a bit longer and less frequent by the six-month mark and by the time they reach 12 months most babies will have one or two daytime naps before eventually these sleeps are dropped as they move through toddlerdom and only sleep at night.

Way before that milestone is reached though, balancing the daytime naps against the night-time sleep is the game you'll be playing and, obvious as it sounds, in general the more your baby sleeps during the day the less she will sleep at night.

29

Do the dummy or don't do the dummy

Few things are as divisive in the world of parenting than the dummy. Some swear by them, some loathe them, some do both and are driven to use them behind closed doors, keeping them from public view like a dirty little secret.

As well as the obvious advantages of dummy use there's also some evidence that they can help to prevent cot death by preventing the airway being blocked. On the negative side prolonged use of a dummy is said to increase the risk of ear, chest and stomach infections, cause changes in the way the teeth grow and possibly affect your baby's speech development.

The recommendation is that you use a dummy only for settling your baby to sleep and not during the day.

30

The controlled crying conversation

As you or your partner haul your sorry backside out of bed for the fourth time in as many hours to rock your baby to sleep life can seem really quite bleak.

Chances are you will have the 'controlled crying' conversation – the general gist being that you leave your baby to cry for slightly increasing spells which are punctuated by you entering the room and either physically comforting them or just verbally reassuring them before leaving again.

When it works parents can find that after just a handful of, admittedly often horrendous, nights they have a baby who settles themselves to sleep and stays asleep – or at least drops back off on their own when and if they wake.

Health professionals now only advocate controlled crying for babies over four months old, and recommend that you do not pick the baby up, but comfort her in her cot – but in truth the whole area remains a controversial one.

31

Beware the squeaky floorboard

Steve, father of two:

"We got ourselves into a quite bizarre routine with our eldest. We would stroke her forehead until she fell asleep, sometimes in the room for an hour or so.

"We'd then creep out of the room on our hands and knees backwards.

"This was fine apart from the squeaky floorboard that we would always crawl onto. We'd scrunch our faces up and pray this wouldn't wake her up, but it always did."

32

Brace yourselves for the baby bomb

Your relationship with your partner changes forever when you have a child.

The terms of reference, the environment, the communication, the priorities, everything alters overnight. This change doesn't necessarily signal the end of companionship, love and togetherness of course – often quite the opposite in fact – but imagining that 'and baby makes three' is the beginning, middle and end of it can lead to quite a shock.

33

The division of labour

Lively debate and even friction about who pulls the most weight around the home may well exist in your relationship before you have children, but it is as nothing to what occurs after.

There's lots and lots to do and it never ends.

It's incredibly easy to fall into a tit-for-tat war where keeping score is endemic on both sides. Regularly reminding each other what a great job you're doing of raising your youngster can help ease the atmosphere, and validating the feelings of exhaustion, frustration and even boredom that you both may have is a smart move too.

There's also an element of giving in to be done here. For you that may mean getting off your arse a bit more and chipping in. For your partner it could mean acknowledging the fact that the house may not truly be as she likes it again for a very long while.

34

Not going out

You'll be coming to realise that getting out of the house with a baby is not a speedy affair.

The feed-change-pack-change-repack-change-time-to-feed-again vortex is a powerful force not yet fully understood by science and is capable of keeping you all indoors for days on end.

35

Talk about cute

As well as general chattering and babbling being on the increase you might think you even hear the odd ma-ma and da-da coming from the ever-changing apple of your eye too.

It's a bit early for her to be necessarily connecting those particular sounds with you and your partner just yet, but it still sends a tingle up your spine even if you might have to wait a while before they really start to call your name every time they set eyes on you.

Months 7-9

36

When to wean

The official line from the Department of Health says that while its best to exclusively breastfeed your baby until she is six months old, from that point on a milk-only diet doesn't give her everything she needs to thrive, with iron being the main thing missing.

Until relatively recently, those same guidelines advised introducing babies to solid food at four months, but it's now thought that waiting those extra eight weeks reduces your baby's chance of either picking up an infection from food because her digestive system is immature or becoming poorly because her immune system isn't quite up to speed yet.

37

That's it, I've had enough

By the time your little one is about seven or eight months old it's recommended that they should be eating mushy solids about three times a day – but do keep an eye out for signs she's full.

Just like you or me, some days she'll be hungrier than others and if she refuses to open her mouth, pulls her head away or bangs the highchair and screams 'FOR GOD'S SAKE MAN I'M STUFFED' – she's probably done.

38

Do the shuffle

Crawling may start with your baby balancing on her hands and knees, sometimes accompanied by a comedic rocking back and forth like Usain Bolt on his blocks.

Alternatively you may have a bottom shuffler in the family, an ungainly but surprisingly effective form of transport which involves using the backside as the fulcrum and the legs as oar-like appendages.

It might not be a good look, but it works.

39

Cruising for a bruising

Once babies can move everything changes.

You'll need to view your home in a very different light – and in the words of the legendary Lynn Faulds Wood, every nook and cranny is a potential death trap.

Get down on all fours yourself and have a crawl around. Anything you can swipe, crush, throw or put in your mouth needs moving. Anything you can open, slam or swing needs securing.

You will also start to use the word careful more than any other in the English language.

40

Welcome to the gated community

Try to live without a stairgate once your baby gets on the move – go on I dare you.

If you aren't a jabbering, twitching wreck by the end of the week as your baby returns to the forbidden but enticing wooden mountain an astonishing 89 times in a single hour, I'll be astonished.

You won't talk them out of it, they won't forget; you just need to block the route to their vertical playground, no matter how hideous it makes your hall look.

41

The terrors of tiny teeth

From around the six-month mark onwards your baby will start the three-year journey to push out a set of teeth that will give a year or two's service before they start to fall out and are replaced by the real deal.

The first series of 10 or so teeth your baby cuts over the next six months have the capability of causing one or all of the following: burning cheeks, red ears, high temperature, broken sleep, an urge to bite everything and everyone within reach, screams of pain as the jagged demon cuts through soft gum, cold-like symptoms, drooling by the bucketful and nappies so rancid thanks to the acidic teething saliva being produced that you feel like calling in a UN weapons inspection team to give them the all-clear.

Winston, father of two:

"Both mine suffered badly from teething, and your heart goes out to them because it looks so miserable.

"On the plus side, however, teething can be used as an excuse for any sub-par behaviour by your children right up to the age of eight."

42

Romance amid the reflux

As you slowly emerge blinking into the sunlight from the first six months of parenthood you may well glance to the side and see a figure that you vaguely recognise. This is your partner, the person who just half a year ago was the ying to your yang, the Bonnie to your Clyde, the Janette to your Ian Krankie – and now it's time to start getting to know each other again.

By all accounts the key thing is to try to keep the little intimate gestures that are the understated lifeblood of any relationship going.

We're not talking about a grope that indicates you may have woken up from your slumber enough to feel fruity – it's the touch as you pass in the kitchen, playing with her hair and giving the poor woman a kiss every now and then that can help you exit the deathly tired phase with the intimate side of your relationship under-nourished, but still alive.

43

Sex and the newly fathered

When sex returns to your lives here are three things to remember.

- Without getting too graphic, new mums can be a bit dry during sex, especially if they are breastfeeding, so bear that in mind.

- Don't be fooled into thinking that you can do without birth control for a nice long while – it's true that a woman isn't fertile immediately after birth, especially if she's breastfeeding, but guessing how long that spell will last is a game of Russian Roulette you'll not want to lose.

- Your partner may be seriously apprehensive about pain, she may not feel at her most physically attractive, after the indignity of labour she may not feel quite the same about her most intimate parts for a while, and she will definitely be knackered beyond belief.

Months 10-12

44

Please don't go

You'll likely start to notice that either of you, but especially your partner, leaving the room will often result in a sudden bout of tears.

Sneaking out so your baby doesn't see you leave isn't advisable according to some child psychologists because it can make her even more afraid when she suddenly notices you've gone.

The only cure is time for them to realise that when you leave the room, it isn't going to be the last time they ever see you. Bless them.

45

From boo hoo to peek-a-boo

If separation tears really become a problem try playing games like peek-a-boo and later hide and seek which can help develop an understanding of separation and return.

If you disappear under a blanket and then come back your baby will understand that you'll do the same when you leave the room or the house.

46

Room to grow

A fact of life is that children absolutely need to develop a strong sense of independence and be secure enough to step out on their own.

So, as ever in parenthood, especially when both parents work, it's about striking a tricky balance between keeping them safe and letting them explore, running a household and spending time with your children, comforting them and keeping them close while encouraging them to develop and learn on their own.

In many ways this is one of the most central challenges any parent ever faces.

47

Hold on

Women tend to hold their youngsters facing into them to protect them, while men face them outwards so they can observe.

48

Daddy day care

In 1968 only 18% of women earned the same or more than their male partners – today that is the case in 44% of households and the number is rising still.

This profound shift in the economic fabric has led to the rise in the stay-at-home dad, with a recent survey suggesting that the number of fathers acting as the primary carer now stands at around 600,000 – a 10-fold increase over the last decade.

49

The childcare conundrum – childminders

Childminders are self-employed, regulated by Ofsted and largely look after children in their own homes.

Seek out someone who has a good reputation, and can be firm and fair without scaring the bejesus out of either you or your kids. It goes without saying that a childminder who doesn't enjoy being with children is to be avoided as is someone who you sense will reach for the TV remote the moment they need to keep the kids occupied.

50

The childcare conundrum - nurseries

Nurseries employ a combination of qualified and unqualified staff to look after children from as young as four months old up to five years and are usually open for anything up to 11 hours per day.

Choosing a nursery takes time and asking around in the local area even before you have children can be very worthwhile as many places at the best nurseries are booked up months in advance.

They are less intimate than the childminder or nanny option but they do offer a real sense of socialisation for your little one, if that's what you think they will need and thrive on.

51

The childcare conundrum - nannies

A nanny looks after your children in your own home, or in a nanny share arrangement at a friend's home, often has a recognised childcare qualification (although there's no legal requirement for one) and can be responsible for a host of duties including planning activities, assisting in your child's development, shopping for and preparing your youngster's meals, keeping your child's areas of the house clean and tidy and even doing their laundry.

If you've ever seen *Mary Poppins* you'll know all too well that finding the right nanny is a tricky and time-consuming business. Notwithstanding having your ideal candidate floating in on an umbrella you'll have to place ads, use agencies and keep your ear to the ground to be able to snare the right one for you and your family.

If you haven't seen *Mary Poppins*, treat yourself.

Worth remembering is that when you hire a nanny you become an employer so it's down to you to sort out paying tax and National Insurance and sick and holiday pay.

52

The childcare conundrum – au pairs

I have news. Au pairs exist in real life and not just in 1970s sitcoms.

An au pair is a foreign national who in exchange for the opportunity to learn another language and a spot of board and lodging at your place will do some housework and childcare duties.

Most au pairs aren't strictly trained in childcare and most agencies who hook them up with prospective parents suggest that they are best used for older children.

53

The childcare conundrum – family

Whether they are reciprocal arrangements between two related part-time workers or a mother/mother-in-law tag team of fearsome proportions, family members can offer low- or no-cost, flexible and ultra-secure childcare, just as they have for millennia.

Of course just as going into business with a relative can be a recipe for unhappy families, so childcare can generate some intergenerational heat when it comes to delivering friendly tips and suggestions.

But if you've got a relative with whom you have a good honest relationship and who shares your general philosophy on bringing up children, then as well as being quids in and a lucky bugger you will also be giving your child perhaps the most loving and secure childcare option of them all.

54

For the baby who has everything

Your beautiful baby is one – but what should you get them?

Perhaps the best present they could possibly receive is you having a day off work and playing on the carpet with them for five hours solid.

Or how about taking a picture on the big day and then a similar one on each subsequent birthday to see just how much they've changed and grown?

55

Horse play away

It's a funny thing, rough play. It's as stereotypical as it gets – a lumbering dad spinning round his delicate and precious baby in an oafish display of chimp-like exuberance.

But guess what, according to scientists this kind of play creates a very real sense of achievement when the children 'defeat' a more powerful adult, which in turn builds their self-confidence and concentration.

As well as letting them win though, when dads resist their children in rough play the crucial lesson that we don't always triumph in life is also communicated in a powerful and real way.

Go monkey about.

56

Let it all out

Being a dad brings some serious emotional stuff to the surface on a regular basis. Loving, fearing, thinking back to your own childhood – it's all deep stuff.

While it's tempting to beat it all back down again with the thick end of a packet of wet wipes, if you can air some of it with your partner you will reap the benefits on all sorts of levels.

Year 2
Months 13-16

57

Walk the walk

By around the 15-month mark the vast majority of healthy babies are walking on their own. From cruising around the furniture they can move into the clean and jerk where they slowly squat and stand, squat and stand like a lethargic Cossack dancer.

Then it's often on to the 'look at me' holding hands stage where with your help they motor around the place sporting an almightily cute grin. From there they will gradually pluck up the courage to take that first step on their own.

58

The time is now

What children experience in their early days profoundly influences how they interact with the world throughout their lives.

They might not to be able to remember a single thing you've done for them in these early years and months but nevertheless it matters greatly.

According to the World Health Organisation a startling array of problems in adulthood, like mental health issues, obesity, heart disease and criminality as well as the perhaps more obvious instances of poor literacy and numeracy, can be traced back to early childhood and the environment children learn from.

This is a vital time.

59

It's very good to talk

Research has found that parents who spoke to their infants regularly enabled their little ones to learn almost 300 more words by the time they were two than children who were rarely spoken to.

Infants need to be given a chance to differentiate between the words they are hearing, so using a more melodic tone with shorter, simpler phrasing gives them that chance. Using many of the same words that come up in everyday speech but in a slightly more hyper-articulate or stretched-out way that acts to elongate the pronunciation of vowel sounds can bring huge benefits.

60

Help me

Nick, father of two:

"'Mumma' was our son's first word but he went on to use the word 'fuck' instead of 'help'.

"That caused a lot of problems, especially when you consider how many times they ask for help or when they become more independent and let you know they don't want your assistance."

61

The importance of play

Play is your baby's work.

Yes it's fun, but in terms of development, when the toys come out your child couldn't be doing more of a job if she demanded a one-to-one, told you she was feeling undervalued and threw the odd sickie.

Show them how to get started with things but resist the temptation to do it for them while simultaneously helping them enough to keep frustration at bay.

Theirs, not yours, I mean.

62

Again, again

Repetition is key.

Repetition is key.

You'll need to get used to doing things over and over again when playing with your wee one. Clap and cheer with renewed vigour every single time an action is repeated because what you are witnessing is your baby practising and re-practising its new-found talents and absolutely loving its own work.

If that's not worth a round of applause I don't know what is.

63

The toy story

As a very rough rule of thumb, from birth to six months toys that stimulate sensory and motor development are the best bet – that's rattles and the like in English.

Up to the 18-month mark experimenting and achieving goals is what your child loves to do, so the building-block, jack-in-the-box toys hit the mark.

As they head towards their second birthday children often engage in make-believe and problem-solving play and can match objects by shape and colour.

The third year is when your little genius really starts to hone and master the skills they have been practising, so you move more into the arts and crafts phase.

64

Word up

Children essentially enter the world of words from the very start of their lives and the more they encounter the tools of reading and writing, the more they learn.

It's increasingly thought that even something as seemingly innocent and simple as your baby handling a book is a key building block for adult literacy. Turning the pages, chewing the corners, even throwing books around is all grist to a very important mill.

By making books part of their everyday lives and not just a bedtime treat you can help to really increase their exposure and therefore rate of learning.

What's more, anything and everything from reading the bus ticket out loud to making them their own little shopping list as you go round the supermarket, all counts, helps – and costs next to nothing.

65

The goggle and Google boxes

On average, British children spend five hours and 18 minutes either watching television, playing computer games or online each day, which equates to 2,000 hours a year in front of a screen of some sort.

In comparison, they spend just 900 hours in school and 1,270 hours with their parents.

66

The rise of the iBaby

Is letting your two-year-old play on the iPhone or iPad commendable or detestable parenting?

In one corner you have the increasingly sedentary lives of the children who are exposed to digital media and the negative physical and psychological impacts they can have on them.

In the other, you have emerging evidence that 'well-deployed' digital media can generate fresh skills and higher levels of achievement and allow children from different backgrounds, creeds and even continents to make connections in ways never before dreamed about.

The problem is, the jury isn't just out on this whole digital/kids debate, the courtroom hasn't even been built yet.

67

I'll be right with you

The digital world has made it shockingly easy to bring work home nowadays too.

You know what I'm talking about – the winking Blackberry on the side, pulling you in like a siren – MUST CHECK EMAILS – or the laptop begging to be opened, whimpering in the corner, a Pandora's box enticing you to release its treasures.

Burying the Blackberry in the sock draw of an evening or leaving the laptop at work sounds easy but in these tough times it's hard to switch off.

In years to come though, the chances of you regretting that you didn't respond to more staggeringly annoying emails on a Tuesday evening are pretty minuscule.

Months 17-20

68

TLC and TCP

Your toddler's ever-growing pioneer spirit not only keeps you on your toes and helps them learn and develop in all sorts of ways, it occasionally results in them putting themselves in harm's way – which often leaves you and your partner as the first line of medical support.

Unless you're a doctor, nurse or medical practitioner yourself (in which case you couldn't have a quick look at this rash, could you?) the chances are your first aid skills amount to a dog-eared card in your wallet which proudly states that you undertook basic training in 1998.

Now is a very good time to brush up.

69

Your first family holiday

Getting away from work, away from the house, away from those black bits that seem to be coming off the bath mat – all these things are good.

God knows your partner would appreciate a change of scenery, having you around 24/7 to share the load, and you might even be able to reacquaint yourselves with one another over a small glass of something cold and wet.

Your adventurous little one would love it too: new terrain to cover, new faces to frown and then smile at, new cupboards to open.

Let's go.

70

Holiday – home or away?

Holidaying in the UK with your kids has never been more popular. You know the lingo, you know the food and you know the water's safe to drink – and for many embarking on their first family holiday that's all that counts.

Then of course there's the fact that your little one can get there and back in the comfort of their own car seat.

If it rains though you will soon have a very grumpy toddler on your hands – hence why thousands head somewhere where outdoor play is guaranteed.

As ever in the world of parenthood, it's your call.

71

The trekking toddler

If the lure of foreign climes wins out bear in mind that transferring a toddler to exceptionally remote, exotic or hot destinations takes either a lot of bottle or a complete lack of marbles.

Extremes of temperature, ropey sanitation and just general culture shock can turn your holiday into a nightmare for all concerned.

If you are planning to travel within the EU get hold of a European Health Insurance Card on the NHS website for every member of your family. It will make accessing healthcare, should you need it, a million times more straightforward.

72

The love

It's often said that fathers truly fall in love with their children a bit later down the line than mothers.

Even the most narcissistic, self-absorbed and selfish among our number tend to be gripped eventually by a feeling so deep in the chest, so adept at flooding our systems with potent hormonal narcotics that it can stop our egos dead in their tracks.

And once that happens don't keep it to yourself – if you feel like telling the world how bloody great your child is, you go right ahead – the rest of us secretly know it's our little ones that are the real stars of the show anyway.

73

The fear

It stands to reason really. When you love something so very much you also become apprehensive, worried, even paranoid, about bad stuff happening to it.

On its most basic level there are physical threats, like cars, for instance.

A combination of fear of the bogeyman and the risk-assessment culture that we increasingly live in is cutting back on the opportunity our children have of developing in the time-honoured way of learning from their mistakes.

Having the courage to overcome your fears and anxieties and let your cherished child explore and learn, while also keeping them safe and secure, is truly one of the most important and difficult of all the skills you'll need to perfect as a modern parent.

74

Ps and Qs

It's important to us as parents, especially British parents it seems, to instil into our children the custom of saying please at least three times when requesting something and firing at least five thank yous out on receipt of said item.

As for sorry, well you just can't say too many of those, can you – preferably before, during and after an event that almost certainly wasn't your doing anyway.

Well the good news is that your child can now begin the process of being inducted into our politeness club and by far the best way to make that happen is by being polite yourself when you ask them to do something.

Months 21-24

75

Check me out

At this two-year mark there used to be an across-the-board health visitor check-up to gauge your little one's growth and development, but in many areas that seems to be going the way of libraries and pothole filler – into the bin marked 'austerity measure'.

If you proactively go to your GP and ask for a toddler MOT though, chances are you will get it.

76

No, no and thrice no

As your baby grows they soon begin to understand that they have the power to make decisions, to register displeasure, to disregard advice and to pretty much do what they bloody well want.

It just so happens that for many youngsters this realisation first dawns at around the end of their second year, hence the terrible twos. Your child isn't being terrible though, they are just doing what you would do if you thought you could get away with it and if you hadn't yet been socially conditioned and handed the fig leaf of embarrassment to hold.

Seeing it in these terms helped my tiny brain to stop chucking out empty phrases like 'Why can't you just listen?' and 'I've already told you' when all the irate toddler before me was really doing was flexing their new-found 'me, me, me' muscles.

77

Let's stick together

The absolutely key thing when it comes to dealing with a 'spirited' toddler is to form as super-strong an alliance with your partner as you possibly can.

A small child can identify a wafer-thin fissure in your collective approach to discipline from 30 paces and in time they will turn it into a yawning great chasm between the two of you – which isn't good for anyone.

78

Didn't they do well?

As counter-intuitive as it sometimes may seem, try turning the praise volume right up during a tough behavioural time, not down. Letting your little one know that a lot of what they do makes you happy and, crucially, gets your attention will encourage them to do more of it.

Rewarding people for good behaviour works too – no matter what age they are. Remember to be specific if you use rewards though, just handing out Percy Pigs without linking them to a very recent action will leave you with an empty bag, rotten milk teeth and very little else.

79

Distraction - your tantrum buster

Look, there's a fox in the garden!

Those seven words served my sister remarkably well throughout the bringing up of her four daughters. All the girls turned out exceptionally well and only two of them have a weird thing about brush-tailed mammals.

Distraction is the thinking parent's way to avoid or curtail a tantrum. On its own it obviously doesn't teach them the difference between right and wrong or that roads are dangerous, but it's a very useful thing to have in your tantrum tool kit.

80

The voice

Shouting is a dirty little secret we all occasionally share, but what can we do to minimise it?

Meet tone.

Tone is shouting's smarter, less socially awkward and better-looking little brother. If you can master the use of the tone of your voice as a register of either your displeasure or alarm at your little one's antics you can save shouting for those rare moments when absolutely nothing else will do.

Then, if you are really talented and you can combine tone with The Look – well you are almost home and hosed.

81

If I have to say this once more

The language we use plays a key part in our ability as parents to keep a calm sense of authority.

Firstly, there's overuse. If you repeatedly use the threat of a consequence to stop your toddler doing something, you will have to either be prepared to carry that threat out at some point or take the phrase out of circulation once it's become redundant.

And it will become redundant sooner than you think, because you will use it hundreds of times more frequently than you realise.

It's at that point you have officially become your parents.

82

Second-best syndrome

Winston, father of two:

"My little girl used to tell me 'Don't want Daddy' and sometimes even 'Don't like Daddy' when she was around two and a half.

"It upset me greatly as I would wonder what I had done to deserve it. My wife would dish out fearful bollockings to her for being mean to me, and it is surprising to realise how easily hurt I could be by a small child.

"I knew it was just a phase though, and it passed."

83

The big bed

There's no hard-and-fast rule about when a child should move from a cot to a bed – although by the age of three most have jumped ship.

Some children will adjust easily to a big bed, they'll love it even, thriving on the grown-upness, the space, the freedom – whereas others may not like it one little bit.

If you are sensing unease, little touches like putting the bed in the same place as the cot was and transferring the same blanket across can really help. As ever, getting them involved in picking the bed and the bedding is also a great idea – foster a sense of ownership of the move in them and you could be on to a winner.

84

Ditching the dummy

I know dummies get a bad press, but for their size and relative cost, they can deliver an extraordinary amount of contentment to small and big people alike.

As for saying goodbye to them, the collective wisdom of those who have done it says that gradually decreasing the times it's used without so much as mentioning your evil master plan is a sensible start.

A visit from the dummy fairy remains a popular way to soften the blow too, with a nice big boy or girl present left behind in its place. Some enlightened dentists – as opposed to the stupendously petrifying ones we used to go to as kids – can now even help you out too by having a place for youngsters to deposit their dummies in exchange for a sticker or toothbrush.

85

Free wheeling

Paul, father of two:

"Best second birthday present you can buy them is a balance bike – a cheap one will do.

"They basically ride around on it and then hop on a pedal bike and off they go, no problems at all.

"I mean, why wasn't that invented decades ago? All the stabiliser trauma we had to go through could have been avoided!"

Year 3
Months 25-30

86

Potty training

When to start potty training is a key question and there are signs to look out for which will indicate when a child is ready:

- playing at pulling their nappy up or down

- following you and/or your partner to the bathroom and even imitating what you do in there

- making a discernible and often rather unmistakable physical demonstration when a bowel movement is being delivered

- actively disliking the feeling of being in a dirty nappy.

When something happens in the place you want it to, ie the potty or the toilet, praise them. And I mean really celebrate, go mad, do the David Pleat dance around the front room, the works.

87

Poo

Winston, father of two:

"One thing you find out when you have kids – they can do massive turds."

88

The strange concept of sharing

What's more un-British than not waiting your turn?

The only thing I can think our children could do that would induce more cringes in us is if they asked every visitor to our house exactly how much they earned – including bonuses – and how they voted in the last general election.

So how should we deal with it? Firstly, try to disconnect your embarrassment bone. The journey to help children understand the importance of sharing is a very long one; a quick chat won't do it and you'll think the penny has dropped many a time only to be confronted by a very unsavoury scene over a small red ball.

Practise taking turns during games and play and when even the remotest hint of sharing takes place throw a praise party like its 1999.

89

On to the next one

The sleep deprivation has passed, kind of. The muslins are all but packed away and the carry cot is now essentially a toy box.

You need another baby!

If you've both decided that you do want another and if you are lucky enough to be able to conceive another you've got a big question to answer: can you afford it? I hope you're sitting down because research carried out in 2011 found that on average parents will spend more than £210,000 on each child up to the age of 21. Like the vast majority of couples who have more than one child though you'll probably do the sums, scratch your head and think 'We'll manage'.

90

Mind the gap

There are pros and cons to whatever age gap between children you choose.

Medical opinion is pretty undivided though on the fact that waiting at least 18 months before having your next one allows the mother's body to recover from the battering it has just been through and also reduces the risk of the next baby being premature or underweight.

In terms of reducing the threat of sibling rivalry there's no doubt that having your second before your first is two years old can have a positive effect primarily because the older child hasn't really developed a fully rounded sense of identity yet so is less likely to feel fully rounded jealousy.

91

Enjoy

This is often a period to be savoured for both of you. Forget the much-mentioned tantrums, you've got an endlessly inquisitive, impossibly cute and relentlessly enthusiastic ray of sunshine in your house for the most part.

You'll be truly amazed how quickly the time will come when you are waving your baby goodbye at the school gate for the first time, a lump in your throat and enough mixed emotions in your head and heart to make you dizzy.

Cliché though it is, you'll never get these moments back, so when you find yourself debating whether to leave early or take a cheeky half day, do it, it's only work after all. Soaking up every minute you can of your youngster is a better use of your time in every conceivable way.

Months 31-36

92

Bye bye baby

Quite often this age can be a time of big change for your toddler, not just because of the arrival of a brother or sister, but also because that big event coincides with another – starting nursery.

With all three- and four-year-olds entitled to 15 hours of free nursery education for 38 weeks of the year many a little one makes their first foray into structured childcare – some even putting on a uniform to do it, which will make you proud and sad in equal measure.

If watching your child playing at nursery for the first time doesn't make the point perfectly, you really are saying goodbye to your baby when they turn three.

Group hug.

93

Knock knock

Making an infant smile is one of life's little joys and when you stop to think about it they learn to express their pleasure at an astonishingly early stage in their development.

As well as beginning to see things from different perspectives and beyond their face value they also develop the confidence to respond spontaneously to situations. As their sense of humour starts to really come together at this age it can be a real ally. Making a toddler laugh as she teeters on the precipice of a major meltdown can have miraculous effects.

Making a point of recognising and encouraging your child's early attempts at humour is a great idea. Create a humour-rich environment by getting really involved in the books they read: there are some seriously funny children's titles out there and if you are stuck check out the inspired nonsense that comedy godfather Spike Milligan wrote for his kids – it will have you both laughing out loud.

94

Food flingers

Fussy eating isn't funny.

If you've got a picky toddler at your dinner table every day you'll know that it can be a hugely stressful and upsetting situation to tackle.

Arranging a daily routine for meals and eating together as a family or occasionally with their little friends can be a good way to change things. Once they see how much everyone else loves sprouts, they could well be encouraged to try them themselves. Maybe.

Making finger foods part of mealtimes can make a difference too as can putting a sheet down and letting them make as much mess as they like.

Finally, don't feel guilty or down if one mealtime turns into a nightmare, go again next time full of enthusiasm and optimism. They can smell a doom-laden situation a mile off, these three-year-olds.

95

And baby makes four

Bringing a new baby back to your home, a home which is now essentially a toddler's personal castle can be very tricky.

You can help them though; there are ways and means of softening the blow and even getting them excited. Firstly, don't be tempted to tell them you are expecting a brother or sister too early. Nine months is an eternity for a toddler and the more time you give them to mature and grow the better chance you have of them computing the news that bit better.

Letting them choose a present for their brother or sister is a similarly bond-inducing exercise and if when they first meet the baby the little mite has also remembered to bring a present for them, well that would be just fantastic and start everyone on a good footing.

96

What's having two like, you say?

We are all men of the world so I'll give it to you straight. It's very hard indeed.

As a couple you become pulled in either one of two directions – neither of which is towards the other. Sleep deprivation returns like a long-lost friend except this time rather than being able to catch a few zzzzzs when the baby dozes through most of the day, you'll have a toddler with 10 hours of sleep in them demanding you build that obstacle course you promised.

All the preparation tips you hear but never do before your first baby are now essential – freeze lots of meals, never turn down help and let the finer points of housework go hang for a few weeks.

What's on your side this time is that you've already been there once. You'll both be less panicky and more measured as you recognise scenarios that sent you off the deep end first time round but are met with no more than a knowing smile now.

And remember, you'll miss all this when its gone.

97

Best job in the world

Jason, father of two:

"When I asked my son what he thought the best thing was about being a daddy he thought for a while and said 'Playing with all the computers'."

98

Baby goodbye

The third year of your child's life can bring with it a change in tone and environment for many parents with nursery entering the picture.

While it's not exactly packing the kids off to boarding school there's no doubt that when your baby starts their first day on the long educational road – even when this first step is a very gentle one – you will feel the sands of time passing incredibly quickly as they come home with tales of best friends and songs sung, of fallings out and races won.

The little one you've carried around, cuddled and wiped the bottom of will be making a big move towards independence and while you'll no doubt feel pleased and proud at the progress they make, it hurts a little bit too as they need you that little bit less. But let's not get too tearful; we've got years of being there for them ahead of us, so let's resolve to enjoy and savour as much of it as we possibly can.

99

Sleeping beauties

Ben, father of two:

"The best thing about being a father is looking at your growing family and thinking how wonderful it is to love and be loved.

"This feeling is increased 10-fold if your children are all asleep."

100

The pretend friend

With nursery here or just round the corner your child will come into contact with all sorts of new feelings and situations as they become even more of a social being, and helping them to be attuned and at home to their own emotions as well as those of others is a real gift you can help to give them.

Also, on the cerebral front your house might get a visit from an imaginary friend at this age.

If an invisible playmate does turn up, don't panic and call in the shrinks, it's not only normal, it's actually very creative. As with a lot of these things, if you are worried about how long your new guest will stay, think how many adults you know with a pretend pal – other than David Cameron's made-up mate Nick, not that many I'll wager.